Out of the Rough:
Women's Poems of
Survival and Celebration

Dorothy Perry Thompson, Editor
Deborah James, Assistant to the Editor

NOVELLO festival PRESS

Charlotte, North Carolina

Introduction copyright © 2001 by Dorothy Perry
Thompson
For an extension of the copyright page, see page 107.

Cover Art by L. Dianna Flournoy
Cover Design by M. Scott Douglass

Illustrations by Andra Whaley

Library of Congress Cataloging-in-Publication Data

Out of the rough : women's poems of survival and celebration / Dorothy
Perry Thompson, editor ; Deborah James, assistant to the editor.
    p. cm.
  ISBN 0-9708972-0-0
  1. American poetry—Women authors. 2. American poetry—20th century.
3. Women—Poetry. I. Thompson, Dorothy Perry. II. James, Deborah,
1951-
  PS589 .O985 2001
  811'.50809287—dc21
                        2001003711

ISBN 0-9708972-0-0

Published by
Novello Festival Press
an imprint of the Public Library of Charlotte and
Mecklenburg County
310 North Tryon Street
Charlotte, NC 28202

Produced and designed by
Main Street Rag Publishing Company
PO BOX 691621
Charlotte, NC 28227-7028
www.MainStreetRag.com

*To Gwendolyn Brooks and Lessie Corbitt Whaley,
the Mother-Guides, and to Nikki Giovanni,
the keeper of the fire.*

Table of Contents

Out of the Rough

As a teacher, I love to tell the story of how Pulitzer Prize-winning poet Gwendolyn Brooks took poetry to a Chicago street gang, the Blackstone Rangers, workshopped with its members and ultimately changed not only the focus of her own career, but also the lives of some pretty ordinary people who came to believe in the power of the word. It is an ancient African concept, this belief in the power of the word to control, energize, or otherwise change lives. Some Africans call it nommo.

As a writer and reader, I discovered early a passion for the words of Brooks, words that seemed to reflect my own life. Though I did not live in a kitchenette in a Chicago ghetto, I did eat cabbage and beans and I knew a man like her Satin Legs Smith. Brooks taught me that there was poetry in my own living, beauty in the habits, language, and rituals of the ordinary people of my own community.

Thus, I was not surprised when Rev. L. Dianna Flournoy, director of Diamonds, a Charlotte, North Carolina, community program for women, approached me with the idea of putting together a small book about the issues the women were grappling with in their daily lives. She saw poetry in the stories they were telling, the emotions they were feeling. These were women coming off of welfare, women who were unemployed or under-employed, women struggling as single parents, and women whose families, generally, were in need of help. The program offered them counseling, job training (computer classes and interview skills, for example), family budgeting, and other types of support.

During the summer of 1999, I did poetry workshops with the women in the Diamonds program, and what started as a relatively small project mushroomed. I saw that the issues showing up in the lines of their poems were basically the same as those in the lives of most women. I called in other women to join the workshop. Some were budding poets, but none had ever published before. Ultimately, I decided to send out a call for submissions to established poets in the Charlotte area and to others across the nation. I am very pleased with the results.

Out of the Rough is a very special book because it brings together a very diverse group, yet delineates a universal spirit of women. Some of the poems drop us into very dark places, both physical and emotional. One poet remembers her

1

childhood fear in a house with angry parents whose words could "sting" like "wasps," another the pain of losing infant twins. Others are celebratory and lift us up with their recall of the soothing hands of grandmother, the strength of ancestors and the importance of an abiding faith in the higher power. Most importantly, *Out of the Rough* shows the indomitable will of women to survive.

—Dorothy Perry Thompson
Fall, 2000

Acknowledgments

I am most appreciative to Reverend L. Dianna Flournoy for her support of this project, indeed, for the idea of it in the first place, to Walls Memorial A.M.E.Z. Church, and its pastor, Reverend Sheldon Shipman.

Secondly, I owe much to my second reader, Dr. Deborah James, Associate Professor of English at the University of North Carolina-Asheville, whose critical eye helped to shape this anthology. Her hard work and good advice were invaluable.

I am also grateful to others who helped in various ways: Jane Bowman Smith, Meredith Reynolds, Eva Dawkins, Rose Parkman Marshall, Cheryl Hingle, Felton Eaddy, and eugene redmond. (Mr. Eaddy and Mr. redmond, both established poets, received special invitations to submit to this anthology and graciously responded with pieces dedicated to women.) To Amy Rogers, Frye Gaillard, and the Novello Festival Press, I offer a sincere thanks.

Most of all, I thank the women in the Diamonds Program for their willingness to share their stories and perspectives, and the numerous other poets who offered their work to this book.

ON LABOR & LOVE
#3

Aunt Sadie integrated
the women's ward of Eastern State Asylum.
She absorbed the blow from a washboard
to her head.

Her husband mad
because she hadn't cooked
took his hunger out the door
left his woman gone
crazy for dead.

CRAZY...

When you see crazy   coming   cross the street   do not stop
to chit chat   ask him how he is doing   do not inquire about
his health   his well being   do not invite him to dinner   open
your door   ask him to have a seat at your kitchen table   and
feed him   better than you do yourself   you are only   asking
for trouble

do not offer him   your love   your body   your soul   it does
not matter   in which order you offer him these things   he will
take them   greedily   and you will be sorry   for you will ache
for these gifts in the time to come

do not become   crazy's girlfriend   his lover   his wife   the
mother   of his children   these are things   you should have
learned   by watching the women   in your life   in your family
pulling themselves up off of floors   making excuses   for bruises
his behavior   sudden fits of violence   the other children   the
same age as yours   the other women   who are younger than
you   you know someone warned you

do not take crazy on talk shows   fight over him   fight for him
with some white girl   with some black girl   with some woman
just as emotionally crippled as you are   do not tell the host
the audience   that despite his weaknesses   he is a good man
that he doesn't always act this way

and this   this is crucial   do not utter those simpleminded words
when the host asks you   why you allow this   do not tell him
do not tell her   it is because you love him   you make those of
us watching   want to slap you   wish you off of the planet

you shame us   shame the race   shame the gender   I tell you   if
you see crazy coming cross the street   turn side ways   let him
pass you   make yourself thin   ease through the slits of his fingers
run   vault   fly   vomit him up   shit him out   if you don't   if you
won't   you'll be   cutting him out of your hair   like day old
bubble gum   and you'll cut   until your mane   is a patch-work
quilt   and you'll stand in front of mirrors   and search for
yourself   threaten to kill yourself   if he doesn't come home
or you'll do worse

you'll stay   stay with him   until crazy makes you crazy   too

BURGEONING. . .

...And you fold the fabric like this I say
It's funny I never imagined I'd be in this position
not hunched over standing in front of a dusty full length
mirror teaching a white woman how to put on an African
                                                head wrap
this woman fighting cancer who once whispered to me
    one day I'm going to lose my hair
    chemo you know
if I buy fabric will you teach me how...
and suddenly it shifted all of it time gender race
yards of African fabric shifted
and weaved together a beautiful tapestry
and this head wrap this device I've used
as my dividing rod
to keep people away
was being used to bring an outsider into the fold and
something within me broke evenly
    and gave way
    tie back the flaps like this I say
folding my fingers
don't worry about the string I say **it gives the wrap**
character here you try
    and without warning another woman enters
    this tiny makeshift closet
    says she heard my distinctive voice
    and wanted to say hello
in three months I will sit at her bedside
while she and her husband deliver their first child
and I can't help but think god is a god of good things
    and one of them is irony
only god could place me in this space with two women
one fighting to maintain the quality of her life
another carrying life her assertion that
things being what they were and are
she had accomplished this momentous thing
was in fact a *woman*
    god would do this and make me think about myself
    that just as surely as a woman could nestle
    a seedling in her womb

peek at it with the fine tuned art of ultrasounds
place legs in cold steel stirrups
push a creature into being
she could also nurture lumps in her breasts
place these same breasts into cold steel
and pray for life to come out of the event
come on in she says you're just in time to see the unveiling
you two will be the first
and she slides red wool off her head reveals
a perfect orb
while the other rubs her bald belly
how could I express to them the beauty
of this moment
how I wanted to hold these two women in my arms
tell them how profoundly awesome this moment
I wanted to cup her perfect circle in my hands
gently kiss her scalp tell her she had
never been more glorious and defiant
tell her I would gladly shave my head in solidarity
until the cancer was gone
I wanted to be mounted with the spirit of osun chant
yoruba prayers taught to me
by my madrina place my hands on the belly
promise a labor without pain
a crib without the threat of death
a childhood without evils some children come to know
I wanted to promise a future
wrap us three inside the cloth and chant on the coming
and going of things and for the delight of things that stay
and so that I'll remember I've written it down
for safe keeping

STILL

this   is how I choose to remember you   with stillness   like
this night   when you gathered together your children   to
listen   for the unearthly strikes of heaven   I   was taught
assuredly that this was the voice of god   creation   was never
a joke to you   in our home

be still   you said   and listen   for you could tell   as if
interpreter   if the creator   was angry   was pleased   or simply
needed someone to talk to   I never questioned   the time
passed   and I became enraptured   by strikes of lightning
the heaviness of thunder   but mostly   by you

and you became   other   the child   I could only create out
of stories   and we   remembered with you   a time when you
were not poor   were not   the place where your husband
rested brutal hands   were not yet the legacy   of your
unhappy hungry children

this is when   I learned you could smile   that you too had
memories   but you   think   think very little of yourself
think you have only taught me   how to live life
                                    black   beaten   and bent
but there is   so much more

you have given me   cotton   and plantation stories   slave
songs   collard greens   and black eyed peas on new years eve
for luck   walks to work   in foot high snow   saving carfare
so that I could eat   you have taught me   how to stand in line
how to march   and how to sit down with dignity   you have
taught me   how to cry   from the pit of my angry empty
belly and how to fill myself   on the possibility of everything
that can be

and I thank you   thank you   for teaching me
the gift of silence   how to use it provocatively   and
powerfully   and in such a way   that it becomes   more
powerful than the shaking of fists   and issuing of curses   thank
you   for teaching me how to   move my body dip my hips
arch my back roll my eyes draw my teeth crook my neck pop
my gum   for teaching me   how to say no   you may not
have carried me   but I am   your own

and on stormy nights of some future   when I cradle   my
children in the easy stillness of my home   I will tell them
all you have told me   and we will listen   and something
greater   inside of them   will give   as I   place a gentle
finger to my lips   and call   for them   with all my love
and knowing   to feel the power of silence.

Janice Lee Liddell

UNTO THIS WOMAN

"Unto the woman he said, I will greatly
multiply thy sorrow and thy conception"

Genesis 3:16

Five children, one stillborn and nameless—
  Bigmama drank hope greedily for the living—
      spat it into bathwaters
        lunch pails,
            and hand-me-down shoes;
    spewed it along a road bound north
  where the living waded in it ankle-deep.
A year after their exodus,
        she shackled sadness and hard times
      to the hand pump of a long
                 dried
                    well,
     combed cotton-seeds
  from her hair and turned her own steps
        away from somebody else's soil,
  her eyes fastened to the Big Dipper.

WEBSPINNING WOMEN

Webspinning is not new for us.
    Mama came from a long line of
dark women webspinners
    who did not spin with threaded
gold, silk, or sunshine like elves from happy
    fairy tales.
She and Gran wove strands of coarse hair from
    pressing combs into tight
vinculums that caught a fatherless generation
    of us into our family skein.
Before them, Gran's Gran loomed
        cotton snatched from sacks that
    bent the backs of many web spinners
        we never knew.

With fragments of a Twi song or two
      her prize filaments drew together a length of
    house slaves field slaves tenant farmers
    share croppers store owners cooks teachers preachers
    thieves a midwife a murderer several idlers and a poet
Under one strong woman's name.
    No man had ever
    claimed them.
We networked long before
    it became a corporate game—
weaving tendrils of
    this or that into strong
    entangling webs/ forcing family ties/
    banding generations
        together forever.
The legacy is mine and already I have
    spent an adult lifetime
    knotting tightly these
    locks on my head.
They will serve the purpose well.
       I
am from a long line of
    webspinning women.

Janice Lee Liddell

WOMAN/BIRTH PAINS

In gestation
     for over a year—
       I am the fetus,
curled up in the lonely room/womb
     of my own making, hidden from the
    acridity of too much life,
        too much trustless life.
For a time I thought
    I was stillborn like the dreams
       we shared in another term.
The amniotic fluid, cold as ice;
     the placenta, calabash hard,
        but it held me;
   firmly it held me
     so I could not abort
       myself.

Jubilant songs and prayers of
     mothers and grandmothers
       known and not known
were raised in my name;
      glory,
      sweet sweet glory.
    They, too, had known these woman pains.
A Twenty-third Psalms and the red of their Erzulie
     served as my swaddling clothes;
    wrapped around my shoulders
     and across my loins.
    These ancient midwives comforted me,
      breathed in me their own unlettered lives
     and I was re/born.

No dirges nor lamentations
     no more despair and no regrets—
moon-eyed wraiths who waited
     in the darkest corner of my small room/womb
    have vanished.
I have been delivered and
     my face is kissed by the sun.

Jaki Shelton Green

I KNOW THE GRANDMOTHER ONE HAD HANDS

i know the grandmother one had hands
but they were always in bowls
folding, pinching, rolling the dough
making the bread
i know the grandmother one had hands
but they were always under water
sifting rice
blueing clothes
starching lives
i know the grandmother one had hands
but they were always in the earth
planting seeds
removing weeds
growing knives
burying sons
i know the grandmother one had hands
but they were always under
the cloth
pushing it along
helping it birth into
a skirt
a dress
curtains
to lock out the
night
i know the grandmother one had hands
but they were always inside the hair
parting
plaiting
twisting it into rainbows
i know the grandmother one had hands
but they were always inside pockets
holding the knots
counting the twisted veins
holding onto herself
lest her hands disappear
into sky

i know the grandmother one had hands
but they were always inside the clouds
poking holes for the
rain to fall.

eugene b. redmond

JACKIE AMONG THE SUNG & THE UNSUNG

Honoring Jackie Joyner-Kersee,
Female Olympian of the Century

Like batons, history's hand-me-down dreams
pass from brain to limb to breath
& suddenly she becomes songified wings
souloing in air & speed & memory,

       introspective as a Miles-muted trumpet

sung by starting blocks, stopwatches, cameras,
measuring tapes & an earthly-astral choir

even as she zings across asphalt,
sand, cement, grass, wood, time zone,
basketball court & water

hurdling injury, setback, rope, tragedy,
bar, stereotype, handicap, statistic & doubt

hurling javelins of hope as she
pushes the cordial dust of defeat
into faces of competitors

tracking & fielding her in/her/i/(s)tance:
ancestrails of Jesse Owens,
Spike Perkins & Wilma Rudolph

       o aerial Tigerette of Piggott Street,
       alumnus of Lincoln Park's Mary Brown Center
       & Dunham Technique, of Lincoln High
       & high hurdles

       raised on rituals of prep, the gospel
       according to Motown, & prayer:
       orbiting/orbiting Cahokia Mounds
       & landing in East Saint Louis
       aboard a gold & bronze mothership
       minted in Franklin School bop,
       hip/hopscotch, UCLA, NCAA,

a quartet of Olympics—the fulcrums of
Atlanta, Moscow, New York,
Los Angeles & Goodwill Games
displaying her lavish lust
for the needs of children,
the sung, the unsung, the wannabe
& yet-to-be sung

high-fivin hand-me-down dreams
& premiering yestermorrow's victories
in cinder-quick limb/o of breath,
songified in air & speed & memory

when Jackie is sung she sings for us all

Felton Eaddy

THE THANG GONE
611 Dallas Court

Wood-framed duplex
Dark-beige summer grass border
Long tinted by early September frost
And gray steps of stone
Lead to the door of a green tinged room.

In the corner there alone with her Bible
Gripped in her hand
An old woman with salt & pepper hair
Slept away in her rocker one afternoon
Gave up the ghost in her best chair.

Found taped in a blue bare wall
Above her bed was Jesus & all
At supper. His long blond hair
a faint white halo
& a crown of thorns
sealed in an 8 x 10 frame.

Found underneath wet layered green sheets
Of rank linoleum
In the window-less john
Directly in front of the commode
Was a letter printed nervously
On crumpled white paper
With blue lines:
> *Lottie I find now.*
> *Lottie I working.*
> *Lottie my daughter working to*
> *Lottie we getting a fone*
> *Lottie the thang gone.*

Found a leather strap
Hanging from a rusty nail
On the kitchen door-facing
No Jesus, an empty wooden cross.

Found in the shadow of a young tree
Was a carefully twisted & evenly braided plait
From an African head.

And someone's always home
But the thang gone.

Felton Eaddy

SOULMATE

for Lois

Sunlight appears
to eavesdrop
on a conversation
between wind & sunflower.
Rabbits hear
and tell the squirrels the story.

Thin green blades of alfalfa
sway to birds' composition
and the daffodils remember
your name,
too.

L-o-i-s, Lois is a whisper through
lavender morning glories,
the coo of mourning doves;
it is like suede dust on the face
of gladiola petals;
it is the opaque blue of rainbows
and the soothing voice of
rain before dawn.

And I will whisper along
with the wind each new day,
your name.

JASMINE

*Phan Thi Kim Phuc, now 22, travels throughout the U.S. giving
speeches, raising money for plastic surgery to repair her scars.*

Think of how you saw her first:
naked, nine, screaming,
her napalmed arms lifted
like wings that would not
rise. No relief, no matter
how far, how fast she fled
or imagined flying. Burns
on her back, her chest,
drilled in, spread out,
so that she thought
she was dying,
would disappear in one
of the agonized rushes
that licked off her skin.
We remember her mouth,
a dark moon of grief.

Nights she dreams
of fire drifting down,
Her body a flower
whose petals curl and grow black
before they're quite open.

She feels herself
buried alive, her skin
peeling off in sheets
so that before sleep comes
she's already bones.

But clouds overhead now are only
clouds. In storms
rain is cool, sweet
water, like rivers
she swims in.

"Forgiveness"
she tells the press,
is her body's reason
to travel a country
where some men remember

in the air
beneath them,
fragments of flesh
floating down
from the sky.

Beauty rises up and says
to the beast,
"The war is over,
the past is the past."

The beast has been prowling
a long time now. He can
hardly hear that voice,
a lute in his ear.

Can scarcely see
through the shaggy hair
covering his eyes
the lilies blooming
before him.
But the scent—the scent
of jasmine on the air
begins to reach him.

How to be the forgiven?
All the grace
is in her.

May our scars lighten
to white, as they do
over years. Let each one
be a blossom, pure
as original pain
transformed, yet itself,
so that we cannot forget
what was there.

A lovely young woman leans
into the camera, hair falling
over her carefully
camouflaged shoulders.
As palm leaves fan
behind, we strain
to imagine the air
become jasmine.

Pamela Plummer

CROSSROADS

there is no shadow
in which to hide
no alleyways or doors
no place for cover
there is no underground passage
or ravine
no rivers lying beneath
stone that will shelter

the sea does not hold anything
the sky empties its bosom
there is no where on this tiny speckled earth
to hide

the snail treks through fields of war
no bomb touches her

and bullets do not scar
the woman that cannot sleep
and worrying me like beads

woman with no tongue and dreams
blending languages
straining to the other end of her song

she is what is left after war

holder of dreams
who has run out of rations
and abandoned camp
who has forgotten how to eat

cutting holes into a reality
that bleeds from her fingers

sewing large patches of fabric
into a woolen wrap

in her village she
was prepared
to heal

always this daughter going
and not wanting to come back

that was her problem

letting everything crowd and feel her
like it was all the same

i have heard her mother's tongue say this since
before i was born

Her throat burning and bleeding
waiting for her to speak

"i did not want to cause destruction
nor tear down my heart
my eyes dry as a riverbed before the rainy season"

"this silence i carried
did not make me woman
but a carrier of silence"

"and the world rushed past me
i saw every bit of it
and no where did i see my face
and everywhere i saw my face
i was here
wanting for freedom"

who will speak it?
who will sing it?
where is the mirror
and the dancers
who move through these crossroads?"

WHAT I SAY

At the bus stop
he rips open
the yellow dress from top to waist
to prove that he can
and for all to see that he can

Some music must be playing inside her head
Classmates chasing paper whipped in the spring wind
Stop and staring
now

She walks onto the bus clutching her clothing
to her breasts like a trampled flower
Sits down beside him—
the one that I cannot yet recognize as a son

She folds into the shell of a shape
A rectangle or octagon
Something that the seat can hold
Something with an edge
But soft
Something that will keep her from falling
into herself

I say,
"When the flower of you dries
Crush it into powder
Apply to your bath and leave the ring
Call on your great grandmothers
And perform any ritual
that images you free"

I say,
"I have no real spells or elixirs
Only a faith I lay down
brick by fertile brick
with no mention of a Law
outside these frames."

"Your life in your hands
is not a reign to turn over.
And this road is paved
with words and wisdoms
Should you come this way
More dead than alive
In search of air
After years of re-rooting"

I say
"Even in the midst of bondage
There can be some freedom
But freedom without bondage
Feels cooler against the head
than fists"

WHEN YOUR HOUSE IS BURNING
(African woman sharing ancient wisdom)

Do not chase rat
when your house is burning.
When the maid is asked to look
after the baby, let her not
complain she has no teeth.
Nobody asked her to eat the
baby.
Know you not, the bird
dancing in the middle of the
road, its drummer is by the
roadside? But, the chicken that is
perched on the clothesline,
thinking that it is punishing the
line, is deluded.
The clothesline is dancing; the
chicken is dancing too.
Do not be the man
who refuses to lend his knife
for cutting bushmeat because
bushmeat was taboo to him
but offers to use his teeth
to share the meat.
As a man dances,
so the drums beat for him.
The smell from the fart is the tale
tell bird singing the taste of the
shit.

Mary E. Martin

SOON AFTER FINISHING COLLEGE AND GETTING MARRIED

from Hattiesburg they moved with her fifteen
cats to Jackson. Their monogrammed gifts, their matching
sets of table fare were tightly paraded
into their peeling shotgun house. For Ann
this was just a stop until New York.
She didn't mind the roaches skating down
her silver serving bowls. It was a place
to practice diction in spite of the odds.
But soon her husband's fascination
veered to major appliances, dwelled in talk
of better neighborhoods.
That summer their suppers,
charmed by the smell
of a litter box, soon stopped.
Fanned by her cats Ann flung
herself loose on the couch with a coke,
a cigarette. The cats skidded
across kitchen counters shattering
glasses and crusted stacks of plates,
licking and pawing silverware behind the stove
while Ann read, patiently allowing
her hair to stick, her cats to rave in the heat
until soon nothing matched.
When one day the cats
shit on the train of her wedding gown
we knew it wouldn't be long;
a short domestic spree
for her cats in Jackson, Mississippi.

FRESHMAN TRIP
for Phyllis

I used to dream about you and Tommy
steering each other under
a blanket in his car. Each night you
returned to the dorm

feverish from the lesson. I listened,
like a salamander slipping in
and out of your view, the way
I slipped in and out

of your flowered A-line dresses, or quietly
sudsed my calves and thighs so your razor
could coast up my legs; I borrowed
to hide my shadows, and you showed me

so much of what I'd never been,
your home hidden near a reckless
country road in Alabama, your church meetings
where the young women smelled like Woolite,

your small gristle faced father
bouncing in his big red truck.
When you first married Tommy
I stopped by your efficiency,

your right arm waving me across
your multi-colored squares of carpet
for a private chat. I followed as the wise one who
had by now careened

through men many times. But as you
listened to my advice, I felt the quiet collision,
my loose wheel still spinning. As I left you blinked
and smiled, slowly backing into Tommy's arms.

DINNER DATE

Caught off guard
by the first blow,
I was unprepared
for the second
and the third,
but
by that time
you were dragging
me down the hall
and
I was thinking about
surviving.

And then
your face was
everywhere I turned mine
and you were
everywhere I had a place
for you to be and
I could not take a breath
that did not include
some of yours.

Dear Jesus, I thought,
if I can just keep my face
away from his,
I can survive this too, yes,
even this too.

When you took me home,
    took home what was left
    of me, my dress,
    and our dinner plans,
I stood in the hall
outside my apartment
and threw down the chute
what was left of my dress
and wished I could do the same
with what was left of me.

Thief!
who stole my breath
and left me smothering
in yours,
could you not have left me
something in return?
Anything would have done
rather than this,
this ghost
that lives where once
I lived.

Judy Corbett

SISTER ROSE

My Lady sister Rose and I share a dream
    of rockers on a porch shaded
    by oaks the size of tomorrow
and having nothing but time and green beans
    on our hands,
our responsibilities shed like old skins.

My Lady sister Rose and I will sit,
she with her glass of water—
    with a twist of fresh lemon,
    if you please,
I with my glass of tea—
    with real sugar,
    if I please,
and talk of what was
and what could have been,
rocking and snapping in the shade.

I'll say,
"Tell me again about the fairies, Rose,"
And she'll spin me a daydream
    of fairies in Mama's violets,
    bathing in dew and powdering with pollen,
    fanning wings that look like the breath of God.

I'll say,
"Tell me again about mud babies, Rose,"
And she'll weave me a web
    of peering into rain pools and looking
    for babies in mud puddles
    and knowing we all had a baby inside
    just waiting to be born
    and praying it didn't happen
    before she wed because it was
    a sin but why? she didn't know.

We'll rock and snap, shaded by that oak
and wrapped in her green fancies,
and I'll say,

"I wish you'd had children, Rose."
She'll suck in her breath and say,

"Why, child? I had yours, that was enough."
She'll think about who their father
    would have been
and be grateful children never came,
    but I'll say it.
"Just for good measure,
you should have driven a stake
through his heart before they
closed the casket," I'll say, but
Lady Rose will say,
"That would have been disrespectful, child,"
and keep rocking—and remembering.

I'll bring up the other mistake she made,
the one with number two,
and I'll say,
"You know, I told you to test drive that
car before you bought it."
She'll say,
"That would have been fornication, child."
I'll say,
"Fornication or finger-sucking, it's all the same to me."

Some of her ladyness will crack in the
startled shade of the advancing afternoon.
She'll say,
"It's a damn good thing I love you so much,"
and we'll touch hands and rock on,
the only sounds the snap of beans
and the crunch of time under the rockers.

Toward evening, when she's talking to me again,
my Lady sister Rose and I will go in for dinner,
and I'll let the screen door slam
    just a little.

doris davenport

C.R. FOR NICE GIRLS & SILENCED SISTERS

she would ask permission from
 a voice on the radio to turn it off
or wait until the person finished
or apologize if she couldn't.

she was so quiet and unobtrusive
she wouldn't even talk in her sleep.

she left left-overs from each meal
so she could eat them cold and not bother
the pots.
she apologized to herself for bothering
herself to breathe.
she died in her sleep one night from stress
because she wouldn't yell for help.

she had a nightmare. the vampire
closed in. before it grabbed her & bit
her near the collar, it said:

"maybe this will teach you,
you should have learned
how to   holler."

doris davenport

HOW TO LOVE A MADWOMON (1.5.81)

from a distance, preferably
but she won't have it that way
she will immerse you in her
insanity drowning 2 for 1
take life jackets for 3 and
a strong swimming arm

ignoring it might bring her
out of it but probably won't
she won't have it overlooked
so don't fool yourself

solving it could work
if you work real hard for
the rest of your life but

don't tell her it's her
menstrual period
too much booze
or she just needs to make love
or go jogging

and in the end, admit it.
when there is nothing else
you can say or do
when there is nothing left,
almost, of you, be kind to
her, and

leave.

Lucinda Grey

OUR NIGHT TOGETHER WASN'T LIKE...

I thought it might be when you e-mailed,
saying you'd like to be lovers but you
couldn't be in it for the long haul and
I said I could barely plan a day at a time
And the long haul didn't sound too good
Anyway and you said since only 16 minutes
Were left in the day, could you come over.
I said yes but when you arrived I was disappointed
It was you as if I'd expected someone else so I
Made the most of it which wasn't bad, technically,
Though you never looked in my eyes
But you stayed the night and held me 'til I wished
You hadn't since my neck was stiff and especially
The hip with the bursitis I can't lie on long so I
Had to turn away and you asked for a pillow
To put between your knees and could I up the heat
Since you were cold. I didn't sleep at all.
And after the alarm went off for you to leave,
I played with your hair but only to stay awake
To let you out. And when you e-mailed
You'd had second thoughts, I left the message
On your machine that I was relieved, had been
Rehearsing my speech and meant it. And finally
The other night after the film series when
Your friend Richard asked us to get coffee and you
Made some excuse and practically ran to your car,
And later when I e-mailed, Sorry I had to rush off,
I'd like to get to know your friend, I meant that too.

Lucinda Grey

BESTIARY

You put my poem away
For a safer day, you tell me,
Leaving me here to contemplate
The dangerous nature of poems.

I shouldn't have kept it caged,
Fed it raw meat, restrained it
With a whip. How could I know

When it escaped it would rub
Your leg, drag a fang across
Your foot and draw blood?

Phebe Davidson

HOLLABIRD'S HANDS

The first time she saw him she knew he
was something special. Tall, Raw-boned.
Big hands. A little muscle jumping at the
corner of his mouth. She wanted to get to
know those hands. Eighteen months and
when she told him she'd had enough he
snapped. He gave her his best reasons
why she was wrong. In court she sported
the torn earlobe where he'd ripped out
her earring and the cut cheek where his
ring had opened her up the third time he
banged her into the headboard for
making too much noise. The bruises were
gone. The truck was fixed by then, so the
mess he made with the crowbar when she
tried to hide in the cab was gone too.
Thirty years later she would be telling her
nieces what it was like. How big he was.
Like a tree or a tractor coming down on
her from everywhere at once. How she
hated him that day in court. How her jaw
never set straight after he broke it. Mostly
they hung on the last thing she said.
*Nobody else ever loved me that way. He's
the only one went to jail for me. None of
the others matched that. None of them
even came close.*

Phebe Davidson

WHAT THE WAITRESS MIGHT THINK OF WITH LOVE

At 2:40 a.m., when the last cup of java
sends its acrid tendrils like filaments of plants
or curling threads of acid up her gullet
to her throat, and veins braid themselves like lariats
on the backs of her clenched hands as if nothing
remains to do but get to morning, she thinks
of her feet, quietly broadening season by season,
year by slowing year, the arch still high and sturdy
as a good arbor with its weight of vine and leaf, or of
stepping from the shower astonished
as a wakened fawn by the blush of ball and heel,
beautiful as the rouged feet of gentle Ariadne,
that ancient woman climbing stone passages into
her history, bearing amphorae curving and cool
as she bears the anodized serving tray, noon to
three thirty, open to ten, shift on shift, week after
weary week, moving in a story of her own.

Phebe Davidson

FROM *THE DEADWOMAN POEMS*

ii

I am drinking coffee
with the deadwoman
in an old kitchen
where we sit
at a butcher block
table and open
our throats
to the hot drinks
and the careful
casual words.

the sun
moves uneasily
through maple leaves
and bowed glass,
making the scarf
on her head
a dull shadow,
lighting her skin
with the gleam
of pale Lalique.

the scent
of a thousand
cups of coffee hangs rich
in the morning air
and the swirl of milk
in a glass jar
is blessing
and celebration.

Phebe Davidson

FROM *THE DEADWOMAN POEMS*

iii

the deadwoman
rises in my night eye
when I am emptier

than I have ever been.
don't you remember?
she asks

don't you remember the time?
and the red veil
of her hair

floats like Ophelia garlands.

one year we gathered sweet-gum balls
from under the tree

filling paper sacks
we had saved from the store
to overflow

and in my frightened sleep
I dream the improbable
grace of parking lot gulls.

BREAKDOWN

It begins with my hands—
this morning
I scoured them with soap,
and now here I am again
in the ladies' room, scrubbing,
then scraping them dry
on paper towels.
Still the scent clings,
familiar, elusive,
dusty, like chalk
or red pen.
I pull white cuticle free,
dragging flesh with it,
a sharp pain, but small.
The air vent's clogged
with greenish dust;
hiding behind disinfectant
something unpleasant.
Like an animal
I taste air currents,
identify each body
in day-old underwear,
its sweat or blood.
Stale ideas, nothing beckons:
through the walls, voices
excuse, question, complain.
My voice beats feebly
on the air.
Going home,
I find myself in the ditch,
watching sun sparkle
on the crack in the windshield.
A butterfly—a Common Blue, wings smaller
than my thumbnail—perches
on the glass. Each underwing
wears a pattern of kohl
against silver powder.
When I speak, my voice is plaintive:
"How did I get here?
Is there a roadmap?
I don't like this place."

Jane Bowman Smith

WINGS ON GLASS

Mourning doves earthbound:
mechanical motions,
the rhythm of a bobbing neck,
they sink beneath their own weight
on small rose-colored feet.
Still, they know the sky
as I do not. Doves step off
into flight, wings sweep out,
clap as they rise,
they arrow to distance.

Yet now one turns
and meets the window.
Only stunned, not dead. She, too,
streaks away.

At twilight, blue light slanting
sketches wings
on the glass: a hologram of silver,
each feather in wings upthrust
strong as an angel's,
a soft oval of breast, blurred cheek.
The image flickers in dim light
and moves as I move.
The bird hovers, ghostly.

I follow the line
of her flight away, out of this house:
into the twilight, shadow, and sunset
partly hidden, entangled
in naked trees. Eyes stopped
by the glass boundary,
I see my face reflected
in the window, confined, limited,
but blessed with wings.

Kathleen Vandenburg

CLICK, CLICK

The needles dance

Her hands pull
together the yarn

Establishing a pattern
Building Less

Creating a Blanket
As she did my life

Strong hands moving quickly
cannot outrun
the cancer

And still the blanket grows
Mocking this dropped
stitch

Yarn intertwining
As I
unravel

No longer able to knit
My life's
Design

Only this can she leave
to cradle my sorrow

A blanket formed by
Dying Hands
For
New life I will
Someday
Bear

But...
She will never see
what I will weave

The bones
I will
knit

I will be
left...

Holding an empty
blanket
and
the memory of
the hands
that formed
it

And the Lid will close...
Click, click

Evelyne Weeks

WHITE LINES IN L.A.

(drawn in powder across a glass)

Someone drew a white line
across a young girl's face
and laughed—nervous and in a hurry.
Butler raised a glass,
Mickey Mouse filled with Gallo
and lit a Marlboro light,
slow and lazy.
A girl sitting cross-legged
on a faded blue couch
giggled and tossed her hair,
while Ska filled empty corners
of the room.
I hid in the kitchen
browning flour in a skillet
and tried to erase it all
with the smell of chicken fat.
Someone pulled a blade
across a young girl's face,
while I was learning
to hate the city.

APPALACHIA 1

We came to this place
in the night,
amid stories of bears
and mountain lions
to enormous ceilings
dark dusty wood
and the cobwebs of ghost stories.
To say goodbye
to ocean air forever,
ignored for its constant presence
replaced with pungent breezes
heavy with November coal stove smoke.

Too young to understand
the way geography
will slice a life like butter
and change the shape of things
until they can never be reshaped
the way they were before
when life had not yet felt
the strain of massive chunks of
land piled in upon
all that is comfortable,
I did not feel the sting of goodbye.

I was the youngest
and followed the rest
to this new mountain home
that I could not imagine.
There is no pain in the first real goodbye.

Debbie Wood Holton

CHERAW, SOUTH CAROLINA

They were three black women, old sisters
living in a one room shack
newspapers yellowed on walls
glued down curling at random edges
Look here's one for Breck shampoo
and another for Ivory soap
caringly arranged advertisements from long ago
Tight pink peonies cut early from the garden
now on the worn, green oilcloth kitchen table
at the end of the room
shimmering heads bowed to be of service
spicy fragrance curling between
the day old coffee on the cast iron stove
Floor swept clean, linoleum
red with marbleized strands now
broken, cracked, snags a stocking for sure
a dull green square here and there, a replacement tile
Sun shines east to west
and through the front door to the
back, the kiss of sunlight rising and falling in its practiced way.

Where's the picture of Jesus?
There between Martin and Bobby and John
the white man protecting the sisters as if by some
magic these images keep the cold and demons away,
and the loneliness
We go outside to the porch.
Thank you for your hospitality
one step is broken, roof in need of repair
unseen birds screech in the pine trees
while tall grasses hide the mating of
insects, the cicadas boisterously boasting
a short life
Three rocking chairs, seven kittens in the grass
kittens for the snakes that come to visit
cooled in the under shack shade
kittens on the roof, kittens on the dirt road walking to nowhere
Kittens bring you luck, one explains
Julia, Julia I have been waiting for you, honey

a hand on an arm then on the hand, a hand to hold
I am not Julia, I say, trying to show kindness in
my eyes toward the roaming memory that is
Aunt Elizabeth's

A sigh, a knowing look between them
You remind her of her
daughter. She died long ago
the sisters say together like in prayer, in song.
Julia. Julia honey, did you
bring my bread back?
rocking back and forth, back and forth
wrapped in memory the day moves on
We sit sipping the offered ice tea
watch the kittens and the snakes
Julia, Julia I made a dress for you. . .
In this backwoods heartbeat
a kindness rendered for relatives
of a friend's friend, a stop on the way to somewhere else
Money to help in some small way,
tucked under the jelly jar vase
graceful peonies now opened by the labor of ants
Elizabeth's daughter gone again
Elizabeth waits for Julia.
Can I find my way back; I wonder.

Debbie Wood Holton

BLOOD WALK

I had no idea that once removed

       those fibrous tumors,
       peony petaled masses and hardy knots
       and tangles that grew like sturdy weeds
       rooted in my core
once cut away

       relentless flooding,
       draining away my spirit,
       leaving instead cramping guilt,
       excuses, Wonder Woman compensations,
       denial

I would be lifted and begin
to soar again in the
sky's vast shine and
the cradle-comfort nothingness
of clouds.

My womb is not here anymore
and this is a wonderful thing,
a liberating thing, an integrating thing,
a miraculous thing

       Me, who never saw a purpose for it,
       only suffered with it, never connected to it,
       saw it as alien,
       replicating aliens taking residence within me
       stealing my communion with self,
       demanding attention
       And when I didn't pay tribute, I bled
       more and more and more.
       Ogun himself could not fight for me. I lost.

I lost, and won *me* back—a tender prize.

MOTHER SEA BATHED ME
(to Margaret, Rosetta, Taren, and Femi)

Mother Sea bathed me
back and forth
Kept washing my feet
back and forth
Kept washing my feet
like I was the goddess
not she
Such humility

The Dagaras say we come
from the sea
Give back to Mother Sea
Bathe in her, but not pollute her.
Talk to her. Praise her. Thank her.
Ask her for help
We talked.
Threw shell and sand and seed
in her face
Gave her our undrunk rum
and then some—
Glad that Poseidon was forgotten.

Derise E. Tolliver

MOMMA WAS A REVOLUTIONARY

Momma was a revolutionary.
      Ain't got a degree in political science,
Probably doesn't know what the Little Red Book is
      can't espouse the relative merits of Marxist, Leninist,
      Trotskyist system,
      but,
She was a revolutionary,
      because she embraced an African male
      and made another African,
An African with potential to love, and grow, and learn, and
      fight
      and make more Africans.
Her sacrifices were for her people.
She stood her ground, even when it was not fashionable.
The days of dirt roads in Alabama reminded her not to take
no mess,
      no matter where you are.

And she knew that in the end, she would be taken care of,
      because,
          that was her Creator's will.

STRONG WOMEN

They came with arthritic hands gnarled from picking and
chopping and weeding and birthing and fighting for a
place for their born and unborn.

They came with tears and pain and the burden of
being "sick and tired of being sick and tired."

They came on big, broad feet, with steady steps,
with smiles broad as the Mississippi.

With sure steps, they walked boldly into courthouses
to confront racism, to demand a vote, a voice.

In defiance, they sat at lunch counters for a pledge
of dignified service and humane treatment.

Their journey began long ago in dusty fields,
on screened porches, in revival "big meetings," in pulpits,
and on mourning benches.

Their voyage continued in the backs of buses, playing
fields and killing fields, in classrooms and emergency
rooms.

And then they danced and pranced and shouted
their way into my life.

They strutted and sashayed
their way into my soul.

They are me.
And I am them.

Judy Yogman

FALSE PREGNANCY

I thought that without regret I'd shut the passage
To the creating of new life,
But see:
Ever since that triumphant operation,
I have been trying to feed the world,
To be
If not a womb, at least a breast,
A fountain
Blessing the neighborhood with milk, with bread,
Raining down coffee and sandwiches, admiration
On every needy student's head,
Piling great tottery bowls of fruit for snacking,
Baking and urging sweets on all who pass
Within my circle;
For each person's journey packing
Picnics.

I have grown ripe and heavy
Dispensing nourishment to those I know,
Impelling energy if not creation
Out of my womb's lost ability to grow.

Judy Yogman

STUDY IN SCARLET

Feeling the dull heavy pulling,
    awaiting the blood,

Awaiting the time not far off when the blood has all left me
    dryer and lighter and subject to climate changes
        of my own season,

Thinking of desert women, crouching on pots,
    pulling their robes in screening tents, unmoving:
        Rachel on camel-seat, hiding her father's idols
            under the veil of custom and woman's shame;

Hearing that African women call the bright drops
    "tears of the widow,"

Seeing the white cocoon: cellulose in spiral,
    the mummy shrouded in streamers of toilet paper,
        white as death outwardly,
            red-brown as earth at the center,
                secret and sad;

Knowing that acts have sequels,
    and lack
        of action is consequent, too,
            and all people
                I failed to create this month mourn at me
                    out of the sunset sky,

So I
    gravid with argument and idea, not flesh,
        muse over bloody batting as if at tea leaves,
            divining faces.

Judy Yogman

IN THE MEAN TIME

In two weeks I visit the oncologist,
strip my scarred torso to be probed, assessed,
talk about energy, symptoms, reconstruction
and read the set of his face to divine my fate.
Next week is the chest X-ray.
Next week they spy out lurking shadows
that cut the breath
if any.
In the mean time the leaves are glorious shards of stained-glass
windows,
the coffee is hot and sweet
and I will be with friends tonight.
Next week is the bloodwork.
Next week they look for iron, liver function, cancer
markers
that resonate with the rhythms of my next six months
if any.
In the mean time my love and I are making plans
to visit children, to visit friends
to visit beaches and waterfalls
in a tropical rush.
In two days my friend will go under the knife again,
will hear
if her keloids harbor a recurrence
and she must ride the round of treatments once again
like my neighbor with the pretty scarf and three days
of work
to four days of low-dose chemotherapy
to scour the corrosion now eating her bones.
In the mean time, I am not dieting,
not saving time, not sparing any expense
that seems to promise smiling or excitement.
In the mean time I am calling long-distance
and drinking wine and making love and listening to brass
bands
and not counting days or years, but only now
because, whatever it comes between, the mean time is mine.

Judy Yogman

HERSTORIES

You, friend, whose next remark
echoes before you say it
my childhood's voice;
whose life is my alternate path's
panoramic map
of a familiar neighborhood,
we connect at the root,
the divergent branches
playing with light and shade
in different ways
but taking
turgor and sap from the identical spring,

the strangest thing
happened to me today.
Can you come for tea?

Dora Smith
Diamonds Program
Summer, 1999

ROUGH PLACES

Ammonia fumes
made me want to throw up,
child number five inside me,
anonymous housekeeper,
bedmaker, toilet scrubber
for the Sterling Inn.

I made sure
Aunt Myrtle got her insulin shots,
ate three times a day—
not even my aunt,
my husband's blood,
but I loved her,
took care of her just the same.

I worked hard
for our girls—
no Lee jeans or Nike shoes, but
splurges for Christmas: red velvet
trimmed in white, blue velvet
trimmed in white,
pink and white for the baby—
all traded for ice—cocaine
roughly killing you.

Nothing I could do.

But when we lost the house
I knew it was time
to go from
the nothing I could do,
to take Aunt Myrtle with me.

She lived to be ninety-four.
I think I can, too.

60

Deborah McCullough
Diamonds Program
Summer, 1999

HOMEBODY

pregnant with twins,
fixed income,
living with someone,
sisters in the street—second nature,

no problem

daddy gone
sister gone,
nephews, too—
their responsibility
my
responsibility—

my head is swollen

i am the homebody,
in this same place
for twenty years

one niece, abused, returns,
nephews, too

my head is swollen

twins die,
i must move
but i am the
homebody,
the body, home
for the generations.

Solande Williams

THE TALK

*LOOK at you he made you cry all over
again and your nose is bleeding endlessly.
What excuse will you use this time?*
That's my mind pleading with my heart to
love him enough to let him go, but once
again I'm not listening. . .

*LOOK at you he made you cry all over
again and you're shaking and your eyes are
swollen. What will you tell them this
time?* That's my mind pleading with my
heart to open my mouth and get some help
before it's too late to do any thing, but
once again I'm not listening. . .

*LOOK at you he made you cry all over
again and you're lying there with more tubes
than you can count and she's so tiny
but she's trying to fight for her life
in an incubator. She's weak and she has no
life left to fight with, so when's the
funeral?* That's my mind pleading with my heart to
stop this pain inside.

*HE killed his own child trying to get
to you, now what to do?* That's my mind
pleading with my heart to love him enough
to let him go. Now I have no other choice
do I?

Joan Abrams
Diamonds Workshop
Summer, 1999

BLUE LIGHTS

In a dangerous curve
they flash behind me, again.
Black woman driving a decent car—American taboo,
especially a convertible,

single parent living in
a good neighborhood,
labeled a threat, put on the list
to be harassed: car bugged, name called out,
phone clicking dead.

But I know who I am:

a woman set free
by her ancestor's seeds,
and you can't stop me
with your arrogant
attacks.
      I take the light
from the Great Divine,
the blue light of the Nile,
of the Beginning. I am
the Nubian, the initial,
the truth so bright
you can't stop me.

Artesia Isom
Diamonds Workshop
Summer, 1999

SURVIVOR

I hear my native drum
        call, but
I cannot find
        my way home.

My tears fill
        the banks of the Nile.

Oh Lord, not another
        baby dead in my
        belly, my breasts
        still full.

Lord, Who am I?

        I am   I am   I am   I am

the lips that kissed
        The children of Israel hot.

I am the daughter
        of the First World.

MY pappy built
        the pyramids,
MY father.

My mother's dead
        and buried in a distant
        land. My hands work
        and work until
        the flesh is raw.

Lord, who am I?

I am the lips
        that caress the breeze.

I reflect off the sun
and give light
in the latest hour.

Stripped of all I know,
Who am I?
My withered hair and
hands don't show
I am   I am   I am,

but my wounded womb
and broken heart know
I am a survivor.

Eva Dawkins
Diamonds Workshop
Summer, 1999

FADE ROYALE

Not the top where his crown would sit
nor his neck draped with custom-fashioned gold

Not his face, eyes blazing wild above the coolest smile

nor the sides precisely edged up every Thursday afternoon

But the knot in the back
Mt. Kilimanjaro arising from the valley of the medulla
The newest new-growth down
strokable as the finest mink fur

I wonder how something fade-ing
evokes such a rise in nature.

Eva Dawkins
Diamonds Workshop
Summer, 1999

REAL LONELY

Alone becomes lonely
    when you realize as you sit in your window
    that no one is coming to your driveway,
as you check your phone bill for errors
    that call waiting is a waste of your money,
as you make plans to go to the movies
    there is no chance of a schedule conflict,
and you better keep at least $10 for cab fare
    because there is no one to call for a ride.

Alone is indeed lonely
when you remember there is nothing to remember
and there hasn't been anything to forget in a *L O N G* time.

Eva Dawkins
Diamonds Workshop
Summer, 1999

REST DATE

Sleep, leave me alone!
Stop grabbing and snatching
at my clothes
as I go about my day.
I
know I missed our date
the other night
but that's no reason for you
to keep calling and hanging up.

Last night
I lay down and waited for you
after you called the first time
but you never showed up
and I waited all night for you.

I'm tired—
    Tired of you showing up on my job like this.
I promise we'll get together tonight
    or, maybe tomorrow we'll do lunch
    (My boss will be out of town then)
But right now
I have too much to do so
Sleep, leave me alone!

Gloria Wade-Gayles

A PROMISE FROM VENUS

(for a friend recovering from a broken heart)

my friend did not know she was a jewel until
he crushed her and those parts of her he threw
into the wind became sparkling stars Venus
used in the light of her promise that love would
return and remain forever.

Gloria Wade-Gayles

THE ONLY WAY OUT

the
only
way
out
is
in
where there are
no
barriers
no latitudes or longitudes
no
measured parameters
no
people owning more than
living better than
wearing beauty more surely than
others
that
is
the
madness
of our world of droughts and monsoons
keloids and polished skin of extremes
that polar us either or
delivering us unto a holocaust
of our own making
the
only
way
out
of this madness
is
in
to the human heart
where Spirit waits
to receive us
and teach us love

RECOVERY

those who hang on to pain forget the seasons that
announce recovery from everything

perhaps they have not seen the sun curve rainbows
after a storm   bringing light

Patricia A. Johnson

MONDAY WE WASH OUR CLOTHES

Through the laundry room window
I watch fat flakes fall steadily.
Snow clings to the ground
Like a long absent lover
Promising to stay awhile.

I fold spring freshness into sheets
And stack them on shelves
Lined with autumn flowers.
I pull summer jewels from the freezer
Bake away winter's chill,
With a blackberry cobbler.

Patricia A. Johnson

SILVER SPOONS

My parents, 79 and 81, lie in bed,
silver spoons in a velvet-lined box.
Daddy's tarnished around the edges,
Mother shines.
Considering their deafness they speak softly
not like when they were younger.
Their complaints flew up the steps
into my room like angry wasps.
I tried but could not always avoid the sting.

Glenis Redmond

I DIDN'T HAVE MY COLORS DONE

When I was a girl
I wore a faded dress of mint green
donned an uneven ebony Afro
danced to Motown
sang the blues off key

uncomely by the beige standards
of beauty in this world
i let those fair lines
not stop me

I danced
sang
until it registered.
deep in my soul
Nappiness = Happiness
power to your own blood
makes one
colorfully
whole.

L. Dianna Flournoy

BLUE DRESS

Mama bought me a blue dress
Like the sky gathered wide and twirly
around my little legs
With a bit of lace at the neck
It was the love-li-est blue dress I'd ever seen
I felt so pretty and pleased with me
When I wore it

Mama bought my sister a red dress just like
my blue dress
But I liked my blue dress better
Cloudless sky gathered wide and twirly
around my pencil thin legs
My love-li-est best dress ever
I told Miss Dumbroski, my 2nd grade teacher
Sister told Mama
Mama took my blue dress, gave it away
and whipped my butt

Kathleen Reilly

THE MUFF

When I was three, one of the aunts gave me
a white rabbit fur muff I wore to church.
It had the head of a dog sewn in blue suede,
soft fur ears, and a pink tongue
that poked out of its smile.
On a ribbon leash around my neck, it jumped
against my chest. At home, it closed itself
and flopped on my bed with the whole
stuffed animals, while mother brushed
my hair, braided tight strands, and tied
ribbons on the ends. I would be clean
from my bath, buttoned into my dress that opened
over a lace-edged cotton slip and—my bare legs,
unlike the pants I wore for play. My father would smile
and say that I was pretty then. The pew squeaked
against my thighs as I sat and pushed
my hands in and out of the puppy muff
that couldn't bark in church, and felt
almost sorry that it had no proper body
but a satin tunnel where my fingers chased
each other, and no legs to run away.

Kathleen Reilly

DARK MOON ELEGY

The new moon bares herself at dusk,
the thinnest curve like a white gold ring,
Venus to the west, a stone
pried out of its setting. How the mind fills in
the shape of emptiness, the full circle,
as I try to count the days of my last cycle.
It is as if the new moon never appears
but hangs, black tarnished mirror in the night's blank,
snuffed, not to be trusted.

I remember the circle that wasn't
the usual blood, my bubble of nothing, my lost chance,
my little nickel. I stared at you
for a long time. You were three month's
futile cells' multiplication,
maybe even alive. Your father came
and left, and hallowed all the sparklers
of my nerves. Later, he returned
every gift. I told
hardly even myself.

Now that I know you will not come again,
I can mourn you, nameless, in my body's
last dark moon, as I wonder
what you could not be—
daughter or son, what beautiful hue
your skin, the soft buds of your face
like his, or mine. I would rather
your failure than nothing, even if
I am the only one to know, as then
I held you unknowing, and let you go.

Kathleen Reilly

MORNING JUICE
(to my mother)

Squeezing oranges, I find you
in the motion of my hands, slicing
the skin to the heart,
twisting each half
until the juice runs out.
At grandmother's, you set
the heavy glass dish
on the table and pressed
until the skins were empty
as cups, lifted out seeds
and membranes with a spoon,
stirred the pulp. You served
it in the red flowered glass
small enough to fit
a child's hand. I sipped,
spit bits of orange, surprised
by what was real. You strained
it for me then, scraping
the thick liquid as it seeped
through wrinkled mesh. Now,
when I dip seeds out of the rich
circle of the chipped dish
and pour juice, thick,
turgid with oranges,
into the same depression glass
that is just the right size
for the juice of one orange,
watch the color that is not
precisely orange climb the glass
and the red flower open,
I lift it to my lips
and thank you for this taste
from which I hold back nothing.

IN THE NAME
(woman as history)

Once, I was full moon
and long-legged corn bowed
in reverence to
pearl colored raindrops,
and honorable serpents
revealed their grafted, scabrous covering
beneath the sun
in the name of darker nations.
Most occasions they simply
slithered about fields;
crooked trails followed
wherever they crawled,
leaving marks of evil
dealings and doings,
twisting narrow-mindedness
into locks of bees wax.
They struck heels of believers
with false teachings
and flimsy promises
that we might illuminate
morning and night, and
the damned fireball would
be enraptured by the monarch of hell
for harvesting swine and flashing
White lies,
and pearl colored raindrops
would be condemned in the name
of their father Yacub
for weighting backs
of brown, yellow, and dark crops.

I was half-butchered
living amongst them.

And it was a crazy kind of love,
equal to the devotion a rancher has
for his cattle,
breeding and nourishing

80

for his own prosperity,
or, like a woman desperately
devoted to a man
whose fingers realize the crease
in her back
instead of the tears dripping
for him.

But that can't be right.
You do love me?
But have bewildered my beliefs
and molded my morals
to do acts of malice
planted long before our birth.
That can't be right
because I would rather
illuminate less
and be silent, than dance
in hell in name
of darker nations.

Josephine Koster Tarvers

FOR LESLIE: AFTER THE HURRICANE, 9/15/99

Nobody ever convinced us that bicycles couldn't be horses
so we rode the Pie and Black down eldritch trails,
purloined clothesline reining them in,
our metal and magic English racers—
real ones, we said proudly—
the good stuff—
and covered that last furlong at Aintree on Eldridge
in record time
in dungarees and Keds and joy.

Nobody ever convinced us that we couldn't fly
so we soared over the bump in Pavlaks' sidewalk
first no hands
then no feet
then no hands or feet,
just missing the maple tree;
airborne for the briefest of seconds,
laughing until we wept
with wild shared rapture,
untethered by gravity or reason,
more wild geese than girls.

This is not to say that there weren't plenty
of things they did tell us. They tried.
Like only sell cookies to people you know.
But they couldn't convince us.
As if we'll get to camp that way, we said.
You have to ring a few strange doorbells
if you want something bad enough.
Besides, you said; it's not like it's the Pike or something.
It's only Richey Avenue.

Nobody ever convinced us that we couldn't have our hearts'
desires,
that we couldn't have the good stuff.
How do you get to Lincoln Center anyway?
In a Checker Cab, Horowitz tickets clutched in identically
gloved fists
and matching suits and felt fedoras,
mine maroon, yours pearl grey.

Where else but a suite at the Algonquin
for our perfect October adventure?
Dorothy Parker and Hunter Thompson and the marathon:
how else to do it?
Where would we go when the wandering took us
but Cornwall and Carolina and Alaska and Ann Arbor and
everywhere?
What else to exchange for wedding gifts,
when we married our men with matching names
but crystal-cased Glenlivet and a silver tea set—
real ones, we said fondly—
the good stuff.
We knew that long before Martha told everybody else what we
had discovered for ourselves together,
before she slipped that telltale slice of lemon
into the dog's water dish.

Nobody ever convinced us
that the rules applied to us.
That love and laughter and patty melts, eyebrows and e-mails
and eggplant creole, trolls and woofahs and books and Frank
and lovers and bloodkin and beagles and cats
and conversations that picked up in mid-sentence whether
they'd been interrupted for hours
or months or years,
stitches in the sampler of our lives,
weren't enough to ward off
the passing of days, the inevitability of hours,
the crushing weight of eternity,
the long last letting go.

Which is a good thing,
because we wouldn't have believed them.
Even if it were true,
which of course it isn't.
There are some ties vaster than space or time
some bonds deeper than blood or bone or biology
some couplings stronger than earth and air and fire and water
and only the heart has words for them.

We always knew that.
Nobody had to convince us.

We always knew the good stuff.

In memoriam: Leslie Cook Ormsbee Brandt, 1956-1999

83

RESPIRATION

In time the emptiness will come to wrap you
like an old sweater
faded, tattered, a bit baggy where it's been stretched
and you will not find yourself constantly checking the mirror
to see how it looks on you.

In time the scars will fade.
Their reddened lips will knit together
as lips do after an argument
and gradually the puckering will smooth out
so that no teeth show.
The sun eventually will freckle them over
so they seem more a trick of the light
than a memento of your pain.

In time when the sheets whisper as they slip over your skin in
the night
you will not find yourself stirring,
wondering if your beloved is coming to your bed or leaving it.
The soft respiration you strain to hear will be the air moving,
the cat twitching, nestling deeper into her form between your
calves,
and not the steady, sometimes stertorous inhalations
that used to match your own,
rising and falling together naturally, hypnotically, comfortably.

In time. Not soon, nor in any measured space,
nor at any pace that anyone, you least of all, can consciously
dictate.
Not because they say "Aren't you over it yet?" or "You have
to move on."
But in time
the only heart you hear will be your own.

FINDING THE DANCE

(for Khensu Nefer Hotep/Kenny O. Carter,
Leroy Williams, and the women who missed them)

Even where there is
no ballroom floor,
you must keep your
mind above the faltering,
the nerves cramping the pit of your stomach.
Go, instead, to the rhythm of words
tumbling from the mouth of the
streetwalker who found her way
into the sanctuary, her shirt
and body limp, her hands
stretched toward the light
above a copse of trees. Dance
with her heart.

Even where there are
no jazz saxophones
climbing heights, claiming plateaus
that make you wobbly
in the knees, you must
hear the melody in the smiles
of children running through
rows of pumpkins at dusk
and the promise in the late
October sky of continuous
symphonies you never dreamed
your mind could contain. Dance
the vision of children.

And when someone tells you
that he has listened
to your life, that he has heard
you laugh only when you dance,
has felt your heart give itself
purely, only when you dance,
you must find it, even
in dark corners, away from
the tiny crystal ball, where the glint
on your blouse is only a multiplied mirror

reflection from the center floor glare,
in the smart bend of your partner's knee,
an old trick he learned,

a camouflage for pain
that started when he was twenty
and fell from a tenement window
trying to reel in clothes on
a frozen pulley line,

you must learn, too,
that stance of grace, the art
of thinking the dance.

IN LETY'S EYES
(for Leticia Ochoa)

there are no hems
turned under, caught
and slip-stitched
so the frazzled edges
do not show.

There are pieces
she doesn't have time
to see,

and jewelry glue oozing
over her fingers, going
where it should not go
until she masters the art
of perfect corsages, shiny stick-pins
stuck to dime-store flowers.

Her sisters (getting ready for brother Berto's wedding) sit
behind a dainty railing
in the breakfast nook, laughing at
her first bouquets, a loop unperfect here,
the knot too loose there
or too tight.

In Lety's eyes
a floral balloon valance
is a touch-me-not, a dream
from magazines she saw
in Mama Ludivina's room.

In Lety's house
she cannot get
to the window.
There is no space
on her side of the bed
unless the man, in restlessness,
turns, by mistake
closer to
his own edge.

Mama, Dora and Vilma
are four hours away
brother Berto, twenty-nine.
The gun is closer.

In Lety's house
the man, snoring loudly, lies
between the door
and the closet where she's stored
pretty patterns, fabric
and drapery mounts
from Mama and her sisters.

In Lety's eyes
guns are sharper
than perfect flowers
and valances, fuzzy pictures.
Guns make peace
and, perhaps,
time for sewing
and for gluing.

BEFORE CANCER

If I had known
those would be
my happiest days,
I would have worn red,
not the modest
white skirt and long-sleeved jacket.
I would not have paid attention
to his suggestion: put on
the yellow duster; the wind may be bothersome.
I would have laughed and gone sleeveless
cruising on the Atlantic that night.
He would not have sat through
one steel drum salsa, his heels propped
on the railing, waiting for nothing to happen,
for I would have had him up, loving
the rotation of his hips, laughing loudly
each time he pulled our arms up, making
an arch for me to turn under, crimson silk
hugging my body, the one knot holding it all together
the focus of several eyes
hoping it undone in the sexy frenzy of mambo.

If I had known, I would have stayed
hours longer among the people
at Chastain, accepted the wine
and hors d'oeuvres
from the picnic baskets
of strangers in the park. After all, they had to be cool
having made the choice to lounge
on the grass, or open folding chairs
from the trunks of their cars
for Rachelle Ferrell and the mighty
George Duke blowing junk
all night long.

And in the interview
I would have told
the radio host more of the colors
of poetry and jazz, the rhythm
of innocence when one is ten
and Daddy worries about the rent

so you can have the Saturday
matinee at the Fox, clapping
To Little Richard's
"The Girl Can't Help It"
high in the balcony
of Jim Crowism.
I would have left out
the college-era sit-ins
for penny candy days
and gingersnap Sundays.
I would have had to tell his audience
what really makes a poet sing: the other
side of storms, putting up barbecues
on the sidewalk so people without roofs
and working stoves can come and eat;
arranging shifts of buddies so somebody's
turning the burgers even at midnight
when the bleary-eyed ones
who stayed for salvaging
come clutching blankets
and wet teddy bears.

On the ferry from Seattle
to Winslow, I would have spoken
to at least one silent passenger, and taken
more notes once I got there: of the scrimshaw
museum, of the native Tillicums
who had known the streams, now deep, dry
gorges. And I would have asked *Are there
no African Americans on this picture-perfect island?*

But I always thought there was time
to come back again, to share it all
with another soul in full flame:
we'd wrap our heads in multi-colored scarves
or top them with batik kufis, take
stately promenades into palaces or mad dashes
into Mexican bars. Salty breezes would call us by name,
and we'd jump in water to our shoulders, not afraid to dip
our locks 'til they were colored Rastafarian. We'd laugh
'til our jaws ached, ask anything we wanted, walk savannas
into the wonderful pain of our past,
then return to our huts to write it all down. But, I thought
I had to earn the right to be eccentric, *renowned.*

I always thought there was time.

Dorothy Perry Thompson

GOD, AFTER ATHEISM

Sometimes, you're the Chacmool,
a stone warrior, jungle-rooted,
resting on your side.
You have watched
the giant movie that is life
split down the middle, spewing
shards of obsidian. There are
a few I cannot see, as they began
with Eve, ancient
and behind me.

Sometimes, you help me sing songs,
thread feathers into my dress

and will not let me pass
hills of pine and spikenard
with no word about them
to my son.

Some nights
you stop the air in my throat
'til I clutch the railing
along the stairwell
and know that it is you
halting my climb to bed.
I dream of vipers,
and lose my children
in a thick marsh
until I promise
to give you the camera
to begin again.

Melodye Micere Stewart

THE PRAYER OF WOMEN

Creator of all the Universe, of Female Supreme
May Dinquesh manifest her life-giving power in us;
Mother of All, may she live as we breathe

Nzinga, mighty warrior queen,
May her strength be evident in our actions,
as Hapshepsut represents omnipotent reign,
May her blood flow through our veins

May Sheba's beauty shine forth in our faces
May Harriet's steadfastness be our goal
ever-returning the truth as spoken by Sojourner

May the boldness and courage of Ida B. Wells dwell in us,
as will the wisdom of Mary Bethune
Let us be as humble as Rosa, but as defiant as Fannie Lou
Hamer

We will sing the praises of our Ancestors,
just like Mahalia Jackson, but be as sassy as Billie Holiday

As we walk the old world, fashioning it anew,
May the wise, unfailing, forthright righteousness
of our Mother's Mothers take pride and glory in
our every African step

May we hear, Lord,
African rhythms, let us live it,
perpetuate it and extend it in the
minds, hearts and spirits of our people

We are about nia, walking kujichagulia
We're walking kujichagulia!
Seeking imani with kuumba!

May the Ancestors, in their Femaleness
be Pleased
Ashay

LEGACY

for Terry

Our meeting is quite
by chance,
as I go about
my routine:
   cleaners
      groceries
         library.
Like the rare red wolf
caged for scientific research
on a Carolina low country island,
I know this path well,
have worn the deep grooves
of familiarity
as I pace
its boundaries,
week after week,
year after year.

It is at the library
I catch a glimpse of you.
I browse the stacks
in search of *The Lover*
by Marguerite Duras.
Mesmerized by the strange
erotic movie of her life,
I am drawn to know more
about this French woman
who took a Chinese lover
at age 15.
Duras discovered early
the primal power of her sex
and claimed it aged her
beyond her years
to make her very old by age 18.

I meet you at the checkout desk.
I stop, feel compelled to greet you
with a banal,

"How have you been"
In my mind, I hear you reply,
"Fine, How are you?"
But you tell me,
"Not well at all.
    My lover died three weeks ago."

Duras' lover did not die.
He left her to follow custom
and marry into his class and kind.
Yet, he told her years later,
he had loved only her.
But you tell me
your lover is gone,
died suddenly of a heart attack
at age 45.

I lightly brush your fingertips
and want to hold your hands,
to hug you tightly
close to my chest,
absorb your sorrow.

I do not know you well
and we are awkwardly silent,
two women
suspended in time
lost in our own thoughts.
But, suddenly,
I recognize you
as family,
genetically bonded
through our sisters,
mothers and grandmothers
to that first of our gender.
            We loved Adam too,
                    You and I.
We slept with Duras' Chinaman
and learned of ecstasy
amidst the squalor of colonial Saigon's slums.
We have labored to bear the children of all men
and felt the caress of all lovers
down the length of our bodies.
We have watched our sons
go off to war

and given our daughters' lives to others.
We know well our primitive powers
feel the cut of its curse,
and become very old
in this moment.

CONTINUUM
(for my unborn first grandchild)

it's like
the hot damp night
that first summer
the gray fox
came to our yard,
teats swollen
with milk.
Hunger drove her
into the open
to nervously eat
chicken bones
thrown into the grass
for the stray cats
who shared the woods. I
woke your grandfather;
made him crouch with me
in the shadows
of our bedroom window, to
watch in silence
this wondrous feral creature
rewarding us
with a visit.

You come to me
like that rare
beautiful fox,
from a place,
wild,
full of mystery.
No more than
a floating little fish,
tiny ten-week fetus,
I am humbled
by your existence,
such a small clump
of molecules,
drawn together
by magic,

as frightening
as it is pure.
You are new,
untamed;
instinctively driven
to become
something,
incomprehensible
by intellect, yet
intuitively known
in my imagination.

You continue for me,
tiny seed of my seed, my
link
to all things and times,
bigger than myself:
   my renewal
      my replanting
         my rebirth
            my release.

Now
I am free
to be the matriarch.
An old, crafty
she wolf,
majestic yet fierce,
I'll prowl the night,
sniff
soft breezes
to catch your scent,
search for
the full moon, stretch
my head
to the heavens,
howl,
joyously and long.
And, I'll
dig a den
deep and safe,
line it with
my own fur
to softly
receive you.

Nikki Giovanni

(UNTITLED)

Talk to me, Poem... I'm all alone... nobody understands what
I'm saying...

Have you been in jail, Poem... a lot of poems go to jail... like
a lot of women who get tired of no good men... Do no good
poems beat on people... Do no good poems say I'm sorry the
next day...

I know poems are lost...'cause they're always being found...
There are Wanted posters... milk bottles... and lonesome
guitars in the night... looking for a poem to take home...

I know poems get neglected... just like do-Wop singing on the
back porch and the deacons opening church with Leaning on
the Everlasting Arms... people forget what got them over...
what saved them...

What are your plans, Poem... Give it up... I hear you're a rap
star now... going for the Grammy and the gold... everybody
singing your praises... Do you ever miss your home...

The sign on I-81 N says: Shoulders Are For Emergencies Only...
ride me poem... I think I've got the blues...

Biographical Notes

Joan Abrams is a teacher in the Charlotte-Mecklenburg school system. She is a community activist and a member of the national Women of Achievement, Inc. She was a student in the Diamonds poetry workshop.

Malaika Adero, editor and author of *Up South: Stories, Studies and Letters of this Century's African American Migrations*, is founder/ director of Blue Media Editorial Services. She writes, edits and develops projects for magazine and book publishers. Born and raised in Knoxville, Tennessee, she now lives in Harlem, New York.

Tameka Latoya Barnett is a junior at Winthrop University in Rock Hill, South Carolina. She is majoring in early childhood education with a minor in African American Studies. She expects to graduate in May 2002.

Dorothy Berry is a creative writer who is also a wife, mother, grandmother, sister, daughter, and investment representative. She lives in Rock Hill, South Carolina, where she graduated from Winthrop University with a degree in English.

Margaret Bernice Smith Bristow has taught at Benedict College and is currently a creative writing and English instructor in Portsmouth, Virginia. Her work has appeared in the *English Journal* and *The Griot*. She is at work on a poetry manuscipt.

Judy Corbett, a native of Charlotte, is a teacher whose primary creative outlets are the pen and the paintbrush. These are her first published poems, but she has published an essay about her father and is currently working on a novel.

doris davenport, Ph.D., is a writer, performance poet, educator and Avon Lady. She has published four books of poetry and currently teaches at Livingstone College. She also enjoys doing poetry workshops with primary and secondary school students.

Phebe Davidson is the author of several books of poems, most recently *Reaching for Air* and her award winning manuscript, *The Plumage of Swans*. She holds the G. L. Toole Chair in English at the University of South Carolina at Aiken, where she teaches and manages the Palanquin Poetry Press.

Eva Dawkins is a single mother raising her two daughters in the same house in which she was born and raised in Charlotte, North Carolina. She attends the University of North Carolina at Chapel Hill where she will soon receive her Bachelor of Arts degree in political science. She was a student and later an instructor in the Diamonds poetry workshop.

Felton Eaddy, author of *Bending Over To Pick Up A Snake*, is a poet, artist, educator, and founder of the Atlanta-based Black Arts Roundtable. Eaddy performs and conducts writing workshops and residencies for Young Audiences of Atlanta, Inc.; the Georgia Council for the Arts; the Fulton County Arts Council; and the South Carolina Arts Commission.

Monique Semoné Ferrell is a native of Brooklyn, New York, and currently is working toward a doctoral degree in creative writing at Oklahoma State University. Her work has appeared in *North American Review*, *Alaska Quarterly*, *Quarterly West* and other publications.

L. Dianna Flournoy is the senior associate minister at Walls Memorial A.M.E. Zion Church, and founder of Diamonds, a job training and counseling program sponsored by the church. She is also an award-winning artist, poet and writer.

Nikki Giovanni is an award-winning poet whose best-known books include *Ego Tripping*, *The Rose That Grew from Concrete*, *Love Poems*, *Blues: For All the Changes*, *The Selected Poems of Nikki Giovanni*, *My House*, and *Black Judgment*.

Jaki Shelton Green is a community activist and writer. She has performed her poetry and taught workshops in the United States, the Caribbean, Europe, and Brazil. Her books include *Dead on Arrival*, *Masks*, and *Blue Opal*. Her most recent collection of poems, *Conjure Blues*, was published in 1995.

Lucinda Grey teaches creative writing at the University of North Carolina at Charlotte, and she edited *Southern Poetry Review* for several years. Her last book, *Ribbon Around a Bomb*, won the Quentin R. Howard Poetry Prize. Her recent works have appeared in *Tar River Poetry*, *Shenandoah*, and *Poet & Critic*.

Debbie Wood Holton is a graduate of Howard and Clark Atlanta universities, and received her doctoral degree from the University of Wisconsin at Madison. An associate professor, she teaches at

DePaul University's School for New Learning. She is married and has one son.

Artesia Isom is a native of Charlotte, North Carolina. She is an aspiring author working on her first novel. Her hobbies include reading, writing, dance and sharing special moments with her son. She was a student in the Diamonds poetry workshop.

Deborah (Dee) James, Ph.D., is an associate professor of literature and language at the University of North Carolina at Asheville. She co-directs the university writing center, teaches freshman composition classes, and participates in the African American Colloquium and an array of African American literature courses. She served as assistant to the editor for *Out of the Rough*.

Patricia A. Johnson, author of *Spirit Rising* and *Stain My Days Blue*, winner of the 1999 Sonia Sanchez Award, is from Elk Creek, Virginia. She is executive director of Sparks Writers' Workshop and a member of the Carolina Writers' Collective. Her poems have been published in numerous journals including *Aura* and *Borderlands*.

Janice Lee Liddell, professor of English at Clark Atlanta University, served as chair of the English department for ten years. She is author of *Imani and the Flying Africans*, a children's book; and *Hairpeace*, a play. Dr. Liddell is also co-editor of *Arms Akimbo: Africana Women in Contemporary Literature*, and her poetry has appeared in several anthologies.

Susan Ludvigson, who teaches at Winthrop University, is the author of numerous books of poetry. Her latest collection is *Sweet Confluence: New and Selected Poems*, published by L.S.U. Press. Recent poems have also appeared in *The Georgia Review*, *The Pedestal* magazine, *Shenandoah*, and the *Ohio Review*.

Rose Parkman Marshall, a native of southern Mississippi, currently works as a reference librarian at the University of South Carolina. She also has taught freshman composition at Jackson State University and directed a writing center at Tougaloo College. She is married and has two adult children.

Mary E. Martin lives in Charlotte, North Carolina, where she teaches English, writes, and develops poetry and movement projects in the community. Her poetry has been published in several journals throughout the country, and a collection of her work, *The Luminous Disarray*, was published in 1998 by Floating Bowl Press.

Deborah McCullough is a teacher's assistant and substitute teacher in the Charlotte-Mecklenburg school system. This is her first published poem – the first, in fact, that she has ever written. She was a student in the Diamonds poetry workshop.

Chinwe Okechukwu, Ph.D., is a professor of English at Montgomery College, Rockville, Maryland. She has published scholarly essays, two collections of folktales, a novel, a collection of poems titled *The Augean Stable*, a collection of short stories, and a children's book. Her poetry and short stories have also appeared in several anthologies.

Pamela Plummer is an Atlanta-based writer and social worker. Her poems have appeared in numerous journals. She was the recipient of the 1998 Hughes, Diop, Knight Poetry Award from the Gwendolyn Brooks Center for Black Literature and Creative Writing. She is currently a student in international public health.

eugene b. redmond is a professor of English and chair of creative writing at Southern Illinois University where he edits *Drumvoices Revue*. He is poet laureate of East St. Louis, Illinois, has won an American Book Award for *The Eye in the Ceiling,* and is the recipient of a National Endowment for the Arts Creative Writing Fellowship.

Glenis Redmond is a full-time poet presently performing and lecturing at universities and diverse venues across the country. She has just been added to the Directory of American Poets and Fiction Writers. She is the author of *Backbone*, and her work has appeared in *Lonzie's Fried Chicken* and the *Anthology of African American Literature*.

Kathleen Reilly earned her M.F.A. from Virginia Commonwealth University, and her Ph.D. from Ohio University. Her poems have appeared in *Windsor Review*, *Crazy River*, and *Southern Poetry Review*. She currently teaches literature and writing at Virginia Commonwealth University and at J. Sargeant Reynolds Community College in Richmond, Virginia.

Dora Smith is a mother of six and a recent graduate of the Diamonds program. She works at the Doubletree Hotel in Charlotte and says she tries to do her best at whatever she does, and intends to keep moving forward in her life. This is her first published poem.

Jane Bowman Smith is an associate professor of English at Winthrop University and has been writing, thinking about writing, and teaching writing for a quarter-century. She has co-edited a book titled *Student Self-Assessment and Development in Writing* and has published poems in *The Mount St. Olive Review*, *Karamu*, and *The Southern Poetry Review*.

Melodye Micere Stewart is an education consultant specializing in the development of curricula and workshops to teach African and African American heritage. She has taught African American studies at Temple University and Johnson C. Smith University, and lectured at Central Piedmont Community College.

Josephine Koster Tarvers recently returned to writing poetry, driven by the twin sorrows of death and divorce, after a twenty-year hiatus. She is an assistant professor at Winthrop University, where she teaches medieval literature and a variety of writing and literature classes. Before the appearance of these two poems, she says all her creative writing had appeared in her checkbook.

Dorothy Perry Thompson, Ph.D., is editor of this anthology. She is a professor of English at Winthrop University where she coordinates the African American studies minor. She has written three collections of poetry: *Fly With the Puffin*, *Priest in Aqua Boa*, and *Hurrying the Spirit: Following Zora*. She is a graduate of Allen University and the University of South Carolina.

Derise E. Tolliver, Ph.D., is a licensed clinical psychologist and assistant professor at the School for New Learning, DePaul University. She teaches about Afrikan psychology, spirituality, culture, and health issues, and has published articles on all these topics.

Kathleen Vandenberg is a doctoral student in rhetoric and composition at the Catholic University of America. In addition to her graduate work, she is an instructor of first-year composition and rhetoric and also works as a freelance writer.

Gloria Wade-Gayles is the author of four books and the editor of two anthologies. She recently completed a second volume of poetry and is currently editing an anthology titled *Please Do Not Erase: A Multicultural Anthology in Praise of Teachers*. Wade-Gayles holds the RosaMary Endowed Chair in Humanities/African World Studies at Dillard University.

Evelyne Weeks is a writer of poetry and prose. She was born in Brunswick, Georgia, grew up in the southwest Virginia community of Rich Valley and spent ten years of her adult life in southern California. Today she lives in Rock Hill, South Carolina, where she has taught English at Winthrop University since 1989.

Andra Whaley, who contributed the illustrations in this anthology, is a freelance artist who lives and works in Columbia, South Carolina. She has studied at the University of South Carolina.

Solande Williams, a native of Charlotte, attends Walls Memorial Church, where the Diamonds program began. Her poem, "The Talk," was written especially for this collection.

Judy Yogman lives in Pittsburgh where she teaches English as a Second Language. Her work has appeared in *Crossing Limits*, an anthology of poems by African American and Jewish poets, and in several journals and small magazines, including *The Forum* and *Green Feather*. She lives with her husband and their three sons.

NOVELLO festival PRESS

Novello Festival Press, under the auspices of the Public Library of Charlotte and Mecklenburg County, will, through the publication of books of literary excellence, enhance the awareness of the literary arts, help discover and nurture new literary talent, celebrate the rich diversity of the human experience, and expand the opportunities for writers and readers from within our community and its surrounding geographic region.

About The Public Library
of Charlotte and Mecklenburg County:

For more than a century, The Public Library of Charlotte and
Mecklenburg County has provided essential community service and
outreach to the citizens of the Charlotte area. Today, it is one of the
premier libraries in the country—named "Library of the Year" and
"Library of the Future" in the 1990s—with 23 branches, 1.6 million
volumes, 20,000 videos and DVDs, 9,000 maps and 8,000 compact
discs. The Library also sponsors a number of community-based
programs—from the award-winning Novello Festival of Reading, a
celebration that accentuates the fun of reading and learning, to its
branch programs for young people and adults.